CliffsNotes

On Nicholas Sparks'
The Notebook

By Rich Wasowski

IN THIS BOOK

- Learn about the Life and Background of the Author

- Read an interview with Nicholas Sparks

- Preview an Introduction to the Novel

- Explore themes, character development, and recurring images in the Critical Commentaries

- Examine in-depth Character Analysis

- Acquire an understanding of the novel with Critical Essays

- Reinforce what you learn with CliffsNotes Review

- Find additional information to further your study in CliffsNotes Resource Center and online at www.cliffsnotes.com

WILEY

Wiley Publishing, Inc.

Publisher's Acknowledgments
Editorial
   Acquisitions Editor: Greg Tubach
   Project Editor: Carrie A. Burchfield
   Editorial Manager: Rev Mengle

Composition:
   Indexer: BTM Indexing & Proofreading Services
   Proofreader: John Greenough
   Wiley Publishing, Inc. Composition Services

CliffsNotes on Nicholas Sparks' *The Notebook*

Published by:
Wiley Publishing, Inc.
111 River Street
Hoboken, NJ 07030-5774
www.wiley.com

Copyright © 2009 Wiley, Hoboken, NJ

Cataloguing-in-Publication Data available from the Library of Congress.

ISBN: 978-0-470-46009-2

Printed in the United States of America

10 9 8 7 6 5 4 3 2 1

Table of Contents

How to Use This Book

This CliffsNotes study guide on Nicholas Sparks' *The Notebook* supplements the original literary work, giving you background information about the author, an introduction to the work, a graphical character map, critical commentaries, expanded glossaries, and a comprehensive index, all for you to use as an educational tool that allows you to better understand *The Notebook.* This study guide was written with the assumption that you have read *The Notebook.* Reading a literary work doesn't mean that you immediately grasp the major themes and devices used by the author. Cliffs-Notes Review tests your comprehension of the original text and reinforces learning with questions and answers, practice projects, and more. For further information on Nicholas Sparks' and *The Notebook,* check out the CliffsNotes Resource Center.

CliffsNotes provides the following icons to highlight essential elements of particular interest:

Theme Reveals the underlying themes in the work.

Character Insight Helps you to more easily relate to or discover the depth of a character.

Literary Device Uncovers elements such as foreshadowing, irony, and symbolism.

Style & Language Enables you to appreciate the nuances of words and phrases.

Don't Miss Our Web Site

Discover classic literature as well as modern-day treasures by visiting the CliffsNotes Web site at www.cliffsnotes.com. You can obtain a quick download of a CliffsNotes title, purchase a title in print form, browse our catalog, or view online samples. You'll also find informative articles and additional resources to help you, not only for literature but for other homework help and for test prep, too. See you at www.cliffsnotes.com!

LIFE AND BACKGROUND OF THE AUTHOR

The following abbreviated biography of Nicholas Sparks is provided so that you may become more familiar with his life and the historical times that possibly influenced his writing. Read this Life and Background of the Author section and recall it when reading Nicholas Sparks' *The Notebook*, thinking of any thematic relationship between Nicholas Sparks' work and his life.

Personal Background

Nicholas Sparks was born in 1965 in Omaha, Nebraska, the second of three children. His father, Patrick Michael (Mike), was a graduate student for much of Nicholas' early life, so the family lived in a number of college towns before settling in Fair Oaks, California, when Nicholas was eight. Nicholas' mother, Jill EmmaMarie (Jill), worked as both a homemaker and optometrist's assistant. All three Sparks children, including Nicholas' older brother, Micah, and younger sister, Danielle, were born within a three-year period, and the closeness in age created a strong bond between them.

Education and Work Experience

Nicholas excelled in high school, graduating valedictorian of his class and earning notice as a middle-distance runner. He accepted a full athletic scholarship to the University of Notre Dame and set a school record as part of a relay team, but he found himself hampered by an Achilles tendon injury the summer after his freshman year. With time on his hands and little to do but recover, Nicholas wrote his first novel, *The Passing*, which was never published. According to Nicholas, it will never be, but the experience began to hone his writing skills.

Nicholas graduated from Notre Dame in 1988 with a degree in finance and married his wife, Cathy, in 1989, a year that would also bring a deep sadness to Nicholas' life—his mother passed away at the age of 47 from a horseback riding accident. That year was also when Nicholas wrote his second novel, *The Royal Murders,* which also remains unpublished.

Over the next three years, Nicholas experimented with jobs in a number of industries, including real estate appraisal, home restoration, food service, and dental supply sales. With little training in medical sales, Nicholas then started an orthopedic products manufacturing company that brought in little income. He experienced two bright spots during that time, though, including the birth of his son Miles and the chance to coauthor a book with Olympic gold medalist Billy Mills, entitled *Wokini,* a title that went on to sell over 50,000 copies.

In 1992, Nicholas experienced more change, more joy, and more tragedy. He sold his company, took a job in pharmaceutical sales, and moved to North Carolina; he and Cathy also learned that Cathy was pregnant with their second child (Ryan, born 1993). That same year, however, Nicholas also learned that his sister had developed cancer, an illness that would later claim her life.

Early Published Works

At the age of 28, Nicholas decided to make another concerted, even more serious, effort at writing. To that end, he spent the second half of 1994 writing a novel he called *The Notebook,* scheduling his writing time around his family's schedule. A year later, while living in Greenville, South Carolina, where he was transferred for his pharmaceutical sales job, Nicholas was offered a contract by a young, new agent with no published novels to her credit. Despite her inexperience, however, Theresa Park was able not only to sell the manuscript to Warner Books but also to secure a $1 million advance, much to the Nicholas' shock . . . and elation! Ms. Park, along with United Talent Agency, also sold the film rights to New Line Cinema.

The next year also brought a mix of success and tragedy: Nicholas' father died in an automobile accident at the age of 54, just a month before Nicholas embarked on a 45-city tour to promote *The Notebook.* That novel eventually spent 55 weeks on both *The New York Times* hardcover and *The New York Times* paperback bestseller lists and was translated into 45 languages.

Over the next several years, Nicholas continued to write, saw several of his novels adapted into film, and welcomed three more children to his family. Today, Nicholas lives in North Carolina, where he continues his prolific writing career and lives with his wife Cathy and their five children: Miles, Ryan, Landon, and twins Lexie and Savannah.

Career Highlights

Each of Nicholas' novels has ranked as an international bestseller. After *The Notebook,* additional novels followed in rapid succession, including *Message in a Bottle,* published in 1998, and *A Walk to Remember,* published in 1999. After that came *The Rescue* in 2000, *A Bend in the Road* in 2001, *Nights in Rodanthe* in 2002, and *The Guardian* and *The Wedding* in 2003. Sparks coauthored *Three Weeks with My Brother* with his brother, Micah, in 2004, and then returned to solo works with *True Believer* and *At First Sight* in 2005, *Dear John* in 2006, *The Choice* in 2007, and *The Lucky One* in 2008.

In 1999, *Message in a Bottle* became the first of Nicholas' novels to be released as a movie. With stellar casting—including Kevin Costner, Paul Newman, and Robin Wright Penn—the movie grossed more than $120 million and hit the number-one box office spot. A movie version of *A Walk to Remember* was released in 2002, followed by *The Notebook* in 2004 and *Nights in Rodanthe* in 2008.

An Interview with Nicholas Sparks

Can you describe your process for writing a novel?

After I decide on a story, the process is relatively straightforward. I write 2,000 words a day, three to four days per week, usually between the hours of 10:00 a.m. and 3:30 p.m. Sometimes, writing may take three hours, sometimes seven or eight hours. At this pace, I finish a novel in four to five months, and the editing process is usually straightforward. Editing a novel may take an additional two months, but for the vast majority of that time, my agent, editor, or copy editor is doing the markup. Then I weigh in on the editing process by revising the manuscript in accordance with their notes—this process usually involves a few days of work.

You're a prolific writer who has a wealth of story ideas. From where do you draw inspiration for your stories?

From events in my life, from people I know, from articles that I read, or conversations I overhear. The question I always seek to answer first has to do with the primary conflict (what keeps the characters apart). I've learned to keep my mind open to ideas from any source.

Several of your novels have been made into movies. How involved are you in the process of translating a novel to a screenplay, and then into film?

Generally, I'm involved only in the editorial process, once a screenplay draft has been turned in by the screenwriter. I might visit the set once or twice, go to the premiere, and help promote the movie. I have no involvement with casting, budgets, locations, directing, or editing. I've also written screenplays myself, and in those instances, I work with the producers and directors to craft the best screenplay possible. After that, my role reverts to what it usually is.

Since your novels began to make the transition into movies, do you notice that you've begun to write with the eyes of a filmmaker as much as that of a novelist?

No. I'm a novelist at heart. My sole intention is to write the best novel possible. I don't think about the film potential at all.

In what other ways, if any, has your writing process or style changed over the years?

On a technical level, I think I've improved my literary style, and some aspects of writing come easier. My writing schedule has become more structured over the years. With that said, writing well remains difficult. It's easy to write something average or even something good. But writing well is quite challenging.

Your novels are set in small North Carolina towns that figure prominently in the stories. Why have you chosen this bucolic setting for your stories?

There are a few reasons I choose to set my novels in small North Carolina towns. First, it's what I did when I first wrote *The Notebook,* and I've always believed that readers ought to have some idea of what to expect when they see one of my novels in the store. With that in mind, I've made the decision to adhere to three general truths when it comes to my novels: There will be a love-story element to the story, the novel will be set in eastern North Carolina, and the characters will be likeable. Then, I make each novel unique through differences in voice, perspective, age and personalities of the characters, and of course, plot.

Finally, I think that setting a novel in a small town taps into a sense of nostalgia among readers. People tend to believe life is different in small towns, and frankly, it is different. The pace of life is slower, there's less traffic, and people tend to know their neighbors; each town has its distinct idiosyncrasies and charms.

When you were writing your first novel, did you have any idea— or even a hope—of how wildly popular it would be? Or did you assume the manuscript would sit in a drawer for the rest of your life?

I thought *The Notebook* had a chance to be very successful, even before writing the first sentence. The story struck me as truly memorable, and I knew the structure would work. And yet, I wasn't sure I would be able to pull off the actual writing of the novel. It's one thing to have a great story, but it's an entirely different thing to commit the proper words to paper.

I was certain, however, that the emotional intensity of *The Notebook* occurred in the final third of the novel. For that reason, I wrote the final section first, and then I wrote the majority of the story about Noah and Allie's young love. I wrote the prologue last. My thinking went something along these lines: The final third of the novel has to be great, but I don't know if I have the ability do that, so I'll write the last section first. After all, there's no reason to labor over the beginning if I'm not going to be able to pull off the ending.

It took a while and a *ton* of editing as I wrote (I remember cutting and pasting full paragraphs and tweaking Noah's voice for weeks until the pacing and tone felt exactly right). But once I had it, I knew it.

At the same time, none of those things guaranteed that the novel would be successful, and I was well aware of the business nature of the publishing world. Yet, when I sent my novel off to agents, I confess I was shocked when most of them declined to represent it. Fortunately, I already had interest from Theresa Park, who is still my agent to this day.

In *The Notebook,* the narrator says that "the romantics would call this a love story, the cynics would call it a tragedy." Could that analysis be applied to all your novels? Is that how you see your novels, as tragic love stories?

Without question. I try to create modern-day versions of the Greek Tragedies. Sophocles and Euripides wrote their plays with the intention that the audience experiences the full range of human emotion, including both love and tragedy. More than that, they wanted to genuinely evoke these emotions without being manipulative. To read those plays is to "experience all the emotions of life." Shakespeare did the same thing with *Romeo and Juliet,* as did Hemingway with *A Farewell to Arms.* Modern day examples include *Love Story* by Erich Segal, *The Bridges of Madison County* by Robert James Waller, and *The Horse Whisperer* by Nicholas Evans.

Essentially, in this genre, the requirements are these:

- The story must evoke genuine emotional impact across the full range of human emotion without being manipulative.

- The story must be dramatic without being melodramatic.

- The characters, plot, and story elements must be universal (feel "real" to the reader), interesting, *and* original.

MFAs in creative writing are wildly popular these days, yet you did not choose to pursue formal schooling for your writing. How did you hone your craft when you were first starting out?

Strangely, I didn't do much at all to hone it. I wrote my first novel at 19, a second novel at 22—neither of which were any good at all. At 25, I co-wrote a book with Billy Mills entitled *Wokini.* I wrote *The Notebook* when I was 28. In the years between these sporadic writing efforts, I didn't write at all. I did, however, read an average of 100 books a year and often found myself wondering what made good stories work.

Why then, was *The Notebook* so much better than my first two novels? I don't know. I will say that it was the first novel that I tried to "write well," as opposed to simply "write." At 28, I was more mature than I was at 19 or 22. I had also absorbed more literature. Still none of those things truly explain the difference.

In all honesty, I'm sometimes at a loss when it comes to explaining when and where I learned to write.

How do you hope to be remembered?

I'd like to be remembered not only for my body of work but also for specific novels. Ideally, I want to be remembered in the same way as Stephen King, who defined and exemplified excellence in the horror genre in the late 20th and early 21st century. I hope to be remembered as an author who defined and exemplified excellence in crafting the modern love story.

INTRODUCTION TO THE NOVEL

The following section is provided solely as an educational tool and is not meant to replace the experience of your reading the work. Read "A Brief Synopsis to enhance your understanding of the work and to prepare yourself for the critical thinking that should take place whenever you read any work of fiction or nonfiction. Keep the List of Characters and Character Map at hand so that as you read the original literary work, if you encounter a character about whom you're uncertain, you can refer to the List of Characters and Character Map to refresh your memory.

A Brief Synopsis

The Notebook is a contemporary love story set in the pre- and post-World War II era. Noah and Allie spend a wonderful summer together, but her family and the socio-economic realities of the time prevent them from being together. Although Noah attempts to keep in contact with Allie after they are forced to separate, his letters go unanswered. Eventually, Noah professes his undying and eternal love in one final letter. Noah travels north to find gainful employment and to escape the ghost of Allie, and eventually he goes off to war. After serving his country, he returns home to restore an old farmhouse. A newspaper article about his endeavor catches Allie's eye, and 14 years after she last saw Noah, Allie returns to him. The only problem is she is engaged to another man. After spending two wonderful reunion days together, Allie must decide between the two men that she loves.

This story is framed by a contemporary man who is reading to a woman who suffers from Alzheimer's. The woman is understood to be Allie . . . but which of her two loves is the man reading to her?

List of Characters

Noah Calhoun   Initial narrator and protagonist; Noah falls in love with Allie the summer after graduating from high school, and even though they go their separate ways, he never stops loving her. When she unexpectedly re-enters his life, he discovers she is engaged. Although he longs for Allie to stay and tells her that, he knows that loving someone sometimes means letting them go.

Allison Nelson (Allie)   As a young woman she falls in love with Noah, a boy beneath her family's social class; when Allie per chance sees a newspaper article about Noah restoring a house, she needs to return to see her summer love, even though she is engaged to another. Allie falls in love all over again and then must make a decision between the two men that she loves, and although she does not want to hurt either one, inevitably, she will.

Lon Hammond, Jr.   Allie's fiancé; Lon is a good lawyer from a good family who will provide a good life for Allie. When he realizes that Allie is seeking out Noah, he drops everything to be with her, demonstrating for the first time that he is able to put her ahead of his career.

Fin and Sarah   High school friends of Noah; they introduce Noah and Allie the summer after Noah graduates from high school.

Morris Goldman   Noah's boss at the scrap yard; it's Morris's gift to Noah that enables Noah to purchase the house that he is restoring.

Gus   Noah's best friend and neighbor in 1946 New Bern. Gus is the one who identifies Allie as the "ghost" of Noah's past.

Anne Nelson   Allie's mother; she does not approve of Allie's relationship with Noah. She is also the one who keeps Noah's letters to her daughter a secret when they arrive; she neither reads nor destroys them, but she eventually gives them to Allie when she arrives to inform Allie that Lon is on his way to New Bern.

Dr. Barnwell   The doctor at the Creekside Extended Care Facility

Janice   The night on-duty nurse at Creekside; Janice enables Noah to slip into Allie's room, even though she is not supposed to permit it, on the day of their 49th wedding anniversary.

Character Map

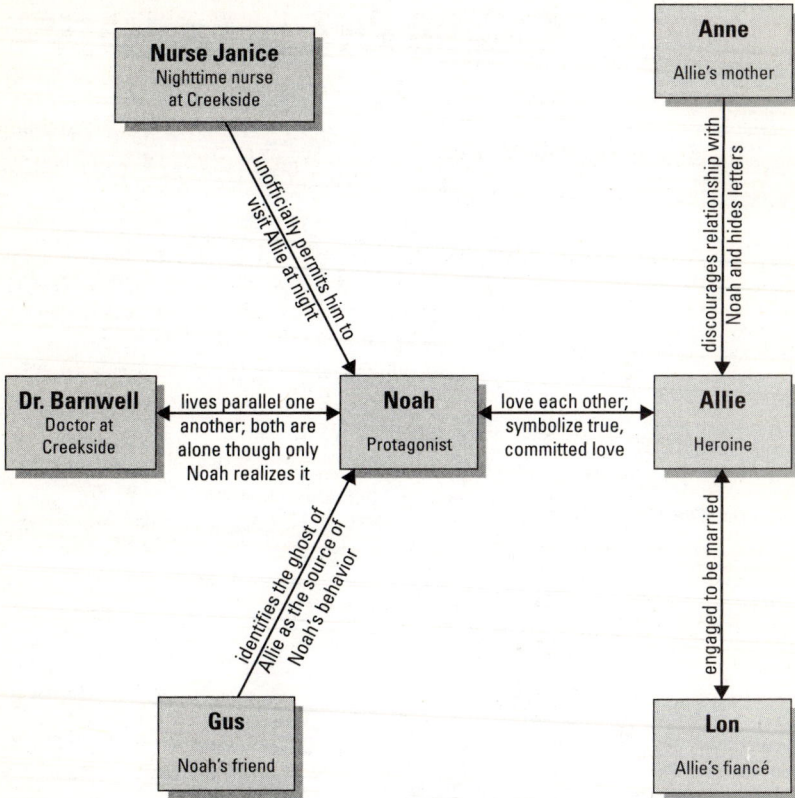

Nurse Janice
Nighttime nurse
at Creekside

Anne
Allie's mother

unofficially permits him to visit Allie at night

discourages relationship with Noah and hides letters

Dr. Barnwell
Doctor at
Creekside

lives parallel one another; both are alone though only Noah realizes it

Noah
Protagonist

love each other; symbolize true, committed love

Allie
Heroine

identifies the ghost of Allie as the source of Noah's behavior

engaged to be married

Gus
Noah's friend

Lon
Allie's fiancé

CRITICAL COMMENTARIES

The sections that follow provide great tools for supplementing your reading of *The Notebook*. First, in order to enhance your understanding of and enjoyment from reading, we provide quick summaries in case you have difficulty when you read the original literary work. Each summary is followed by commentary: literary devices, character analyses, themes, and so on. Keep in mind that the interpretations here are solely those of the author of this study guide and are used to jumpstart your thinking about the work. No single interpretation of a complex work like *The Notebook* is infallible or exhaustive, and you'll likely find that you interpret portions of the work differently from the author of this study guide. Read the original work and determine your own interpretations, referring to these notes for supplemental meanings only.

Dedication

The Notebook is dedicated "to Cathy," a person identified as "my wife and my friend."

Commentary

The dedication to *The Notebook* mirrors everything else about the novel: It is straightforward and seemingly simplistic. In fact, many, if not most, readers probably skip the dedication entirely. Yet, the dedication establishes the tone for the entire text, not only mentioning the three most important words—*love, wife,* and *friend*—but connecting the three in what is clearly the most important person in the life of Nicholas Sparks. In interviews, Sparks admitted that the genesis of *The Notebook* was from his own family history, and in the dedication of his debut novel, he confirms for the entire reading population the significant effect his wife has on his own life. *The Notebook* is not only the love story of Noah and Allie, but also it is essentially the love story of Nicholas and Cathy.

Miracles

Summary

The Notebook opens with an unnamed narrator asking "Who am I?" Readers realize that this narrator is also an older person because 30 years ago the narrator's daughter knitted the sweater that is being worn; soon after, readers learn that this nameless narrator is 80 years old. The narrator provides two choices for the reader, claiming that this narrative is either a love story or a tragedy, depending on whether you are a romantic or a cynic, and yet, the narrator considers it a little bit of both.

Without revealing specifics, the narrator states that the life path that the narrator has chosen to follow was indeed a choice, and the major difficulties, or problems, began three years ago. The mention of both a nurse and crying suggest a nursing home or some other extended care facility, and when the narrator quotes a nurse, the narrator's gender is finally revealed—he is a male.

He walks down the hall into a room and chats with the two nurses who are in the room. Then he settles in to his usual chair, knowing that the crying will soon stop. The woman he is visiting does not know who the narrator is. The narrator mentions both God and the power of prayer. And then he starts to read from a notebook, in hopes that the miracle will again prevail.

From Nicholas

1. Can you describe how the idea for *The Notebook* came to you?

The novel was inspired by my wife's grandparents. In many ways, Noah and Allie's story paralleled the story of her grandparents: They'd met as teenagers, moved away from each other only to reunite years later on the verge of her wedding to another man. They lived a long and happy life together until one of them developed dementia. Theirs was both a wonderful and tragic story, and most importantly, it was a story that I thought I could write. The relatively simple story embraced two major characters and two major settings, and yet the story struck me as having infinite possibilities from the very beginning. Because I had such confidence in the story, I devoted most of my writing time to the literary style, in order to make Noah's voice and tone as memorable as possible.

Commentary

Style & Language

The title of the opening chapter establishes the motif of miracles. Although readers are not aware of which specific miracle the title refers, a safe assumption is that it has something to do with the person to whom the narrator is reading from the notebook—presumably because this notebook is the one mentioned in the title and has some important significance. Throughout *The Notebook,* a number of different miracles occur, and all of them involve either one or both of the two main characters: Noah and/or Allie.

Theme

The title of the chapter is followed by two questions. The opening question "Who am I?" establishes the importance of gaining an understanding of self. This begins the development of one of the most important thematic topics of the novel, and this quest for self-understanding also serves as an important part of the development of the main characters.

This understanding of self is also explored throughout Walt Whitman's collection of poetry, *Leaves of Grass,* which serves as an important intertext for *The Notebook.* The second question asks "How . . . will this story end?" The question specifically refers to the narrator's story but also symbolizes the story of everyone's life and the uncertainty that people face during their existence.

Theme

The narrator's uncertainty in regards to his future introduces another thematic topic—that is, the relationship between fate and free will. Oftentimes, people view these two as contrasting, mutually exclusive ideas, yet *The Notebook* seems to suggest that people exercise free will even as they move toward their fate. People commit actions, and these actions have consequences. What role, if any, fate has in relation to these actions and consequences is explored throughout the remainder of the novel.

Style & Language

The conversational tone established by the narrator reveals the personal nature of the narrative and serves to pull in the reader by creating a sense of intimacy. This informal tone enables readers to connect with the narrator, becoming emotionally invested in the story. The informal tone and easy-to-read narrative are deceptive because the ideas and characters in *The Notebook* are not as simplistic. Sparks' style enables him to both reach and connect with a wide audience.

The narrator repeats the word "common," referring both to himself as a man and his thoughts. This word usually has a neutral if not negative connotation; however, in this chapter, the word occurs immediately after the narrator compares his relationship to a blue-chip stock, a stock whose success is virtually guaranteed over time. The word "common" is also an investment term (blue chip stocks are actually well-regarded shares of common stock).

Therefore, Sparks not only continues his metaphor, he develops the character of the narrator, demonstrating a degree of modesty as well as insight. The narrator is one who "loved another with all my heart and soul" and for him "that has always been enough." Clearly, love is not common at all. And *The Notebook* explores the nature of an uncommon love. At this time, the narrator does not say all of this, yet readers are able to infer this information. *The Notebook* is an exploration of enduring, committed love.

By the narrator's own admission, his story is both a love story and a tragedy—in fact, it is better to identify it as a tragic love story, one along the lines of *Romeo and Juliet*. And although similarities exist, the parallels are neither perfect nor identical. Yet, texts do not have to be identical to influence one another.

Another important repetition is the narrator's use of the word *path*. Not only does it emphasize the walk of life that everyone takes, it establishes the mood, or atmosphere, of the text. A sense of acceptance and strong sense of faith permeate the opening pages of *The Notebook* and continue throughout the novel.

A number of important images take place in this opening chapter. The narrator compares himself to an "old party balloon." This image works on two levels, indicating both the physical as well as the emotional and spiritual well being of the narrator. He is currently only a shell of his former self. The chair that has "come to be shaped like me" indicates the amount of time that he has spent sitting in the chair, presumably reading the notebook, the one that has been read "a hundred times." This detail appears to be a statement of fact and not of hyperbole. Another indication of the amount of time that he has spent here is the familiarity the narrator has with the nurses.

The attitude of narrator reveals an important thematic statement of *The Notebook*. The narrator states, "A person can get used to anything, if given enough time." On the surface, this sentence could have both positive and negative connotations; however, based on the context of the chapter, this indication is definitely a positive one. The narrator is a character who is clearly making the best of a bad situation. He seems to have accepted the conditions of his life.

Just as the nurses "say nothing directly to me," the narrator is not saying many things directly to the readers. The indirection is a stylistic technique used by Nicholas Sparks to build suspense. One of the most important things that is not stated directly but is easily inferred is the fact that the patient to whom the narrator is reading is suffering from Alzheimer's. But the narrator has already revealed himself to be a man of faith and then states that he believes "anything is possible" and that "science is not the total answer," reinforcing the idea of fate, free will, and miracles. The repetition of the word *miracle* echoes the title of the chapter while simultaneously emphasizing its importance. *Miracle* as a word also has religious connotations, another important motif used to develop both character and theme.

The single sentence used to end the chapter focuses readers on the hope that the narrator has, connecting readers to the desire he has for yet another miracle associated with the notebook.

This first chapter has two primary purposes: to establish the frame narrative and to build both suspense and mystery. This chapter introduces an 80-year-old narrator whose story is in the present. This narrative surrounds the flashback story that is told in subsequent chapters. Suspense and mystery is created through a variety of means—the nameless narrator (who is he?), the unknown person to whom he is reading, the mentioning (without identifying) of a problem, and the notebook itself. Clearly, this introductory chapter raises more questions than it answers.

Readers are not immediately aware of what is thematically and symbolically significant and cannot possibly fully understand and appreciate their inclusion in the first chapter until rereading the chapter after completing the entire novel.

Glossary

blue-chip stock   stocks of high-quality, financially-sound corporations; the term suggests a safe investment

listless   indifferent, spiritless

Ghosts

Summary

The narrative flashes back to October 1946 and a character named Noah Calhoun. Noah enjoys thinking about nothing in particular in the evenings after a hard day at work repairing the house he purchased in New Bern, North Carolina. The house was originally built in 1772, and Noah has spent the past eleven months fixing it up.

Both his guitar and his memories of his father occupy Noah's time. Noah does not currently have a job, but he is not particularly concerned with finding one because he still has a few months worth of savings left. Noah has a hound dog, Clem—short for Clementine—and at 31 years old, he is beginning to feel lonely. He has not dated since he returned to New Bern.

Memories of his father include the mention of "God's music," a reference to the sounds of nature, the sounds that enabled Noah to help keep his sanity during the chaos and confusion during the time he spent fighting in a war. After drinking his tea, Noah gets his copy of Walt Whitman's *Leaves of Grass,* and quotes an entire poem.

From Nicholas

Noah's dog, Clementine, is missing a leg. Did you see this as a metaphor for the part of Noah that's missing; was it to show that Noah has a great capacity for love and acceptance; or what is simply an interesting detail to make Clem memorable?

The missing leg was meant to be a metaphor of sorts: Both Noah and Clementine were wounded. Noah's love and companionship ensured that Clementine was able to overcome her "wound," just as Allie's love ensured that Noah would heal as well.

Readers learn that although Noah has been away from New Bern for 14 years, he still considers it home. His newest best friend is his neighbor Gus, a 70-year-old black man who lives down the street. Often they visit, play music, and share a drink on Noah's porch.

The reason for Noah not marrying is not stated. But one of the reasons may be that he missed the opportunity to marry the one girl he would have liked to have married, his summer love of 1932, the year of his high school graduation. Fin and Sarah, two of his friends, introduced Noah to her—the woman he would want to spend the rest of his life with. Not only do the two of them become inseparable that summer, they share their virginity with one another. Noah even points out the house that he plans on buying and restoring for them. When Noah talks to Gus about the one who got away, Gus proclaims her to be the "ghost" that Noah is running from, equating the word ghost with the word "memory."

From Nicholas

Even though Noah's father has passed away by 1946, Noah refers to him often and describes the lessons his father taught him. Your own father passed away the same year *The Notebook* was published. Is Noah's relationship with his father similar to your relationship with your father?

Not really. My dad was a quiet intellectual, a professor who taught business and public administration, and a kind man. But he wasn't the type of father who took an active role in the lives of his children. Often, when I was struggling with a problem, I'd go to him, but he seldom, if ever, offered advice. Instead, he asked me questions, prodding me into discovering the answer on my own. He was a father and a mentor, but our relationship was different than the relationship I imagined that Noah had with his father.

The chapter then shifts to the story of Allie. She wonders if she has made the right decision, leaving her fiancé Lon, lying to Lon about the reason for her trip, a trip that requires traveling over two hours from Raleigh to New Bern. Lon and the lady with the secret had known each other for four years and are both socially matched. He is a lawyer. But she needs to confront her own ghost, her own memory of her summer love, and she finds that it is impossible to explain this to Lon.

The narrative shifts back to Noah and his work day. During this time the narrator reveals that Noah's father was the person responsible for instilling a love of poetry—particularly Whitman and Tennyson—in his son. When Noah remembers his love, he finally mentions her name—Allie. Fin had predicted that Noah and Allie would fall in love. He also predicted it would not work out. And Fin was correct on both accounts. Although Noah wrote her letters after Allie left at the end of the summer, the letters were never answered. Noah eventually leaves New Bern, for two reasons: to help him forget Allie and to find significant employment. He eventually settles in New Jersey, working in a scrap yard for Morris Goldman.

From Nicholas

Family is deeply important to Noah, yet he feels comfortable living alone, with few friends and no nearby relatives. Does this blend of comfort being alone, yet with a respect for family, speak to his maturity?

As the novel flashes back to 1946, Noah could best be described as "emotionally wounded." In the first draft of the novel, I explored Noah's war-time experiences, including his involvement in the Battle of the Bulge, and I envisioned him as a bit scarred from the experience. In the end, however, I ended up cutting those pages. I felt they added little to the overall story, since his demeanor and lifestyle prior to Allie's return suggests the emotional wounds he'd suffered in his past. His war-time experience, the recent loss of a father he loved, and lingering memories of Allie, made Noah retreat within himself, and he found comfort in the steady act of repairing an old country home. Like everyone in the world, he was molded and formed by his history, and by rebuilding the country house, he was in essence trying to rebuild his life into something that made sense again.

Three years after he sent the last letter, Noah went to Winston Salem in an attempt to find Allie; however, her family had moved, and her father had left the company for whom he had worked, and there was no forwarding information. Eventually Noah dates a few women and even gets serious with one, but no one can fill the void in his heart left by Allie.

When World War II breaks out, Noah enlists and spends three years in the service. Just as he was getting discharged, Noah finds out that Morris Goldman had died, and the liquidation of his assets provided Noah, who received from Morris the gift of a small percentage of the scrap yard, with almost $70,000. Noah used this money to purchase the house he was refinishing. Noah's father died from pneumonia about a month after Noah showed him the house and explained his plans for the remodeling. As Noah is settling in with a Budweiser and a collection of poetry by Dylan Thomas, the narrative again shifts back to Allie.

The second poem quoted in the chapter is Allie's remembrance of Noah reading to her. She recalls the poem and many other fond memories as she travels to his house. When she arrives, he comes off the porch, moving toward her car, until he identifies her. Then he stops cold in his tracks.

From Nicholas

Noah says that perfect love "changed him forever." Yet that love ended suddenly, inexplicably? Why did the loss of such a perfect love not make him bitter and cold?

Because love of any kind leaves ripples, and Noah found it easier to find beauty in the ripples than sadness. Underlying that notion is the belief that true love is a gift we not only give to another, but to ourselves.

Commentary

The opening sentence of the second chapter provides the setting of the inner-story of the frame narrative. Although it is not stated directly, readers have a sense that this story is the one that is recorded in the pages of the notebook.

Literary Device

The narrative point of view shifts from a first person to a third person perspective. An omniscient narrator begins telling the love story of Noah and Allie. This choice of narrator is significant, for it enables readers to know what is happening in the minds of both main characters.

At the beginning, the text does not directly state that Noah's father is dead, nor does it state that Noah served in the war, though astute readers will infer both of these things. These examples illustrate Sparks' style of narrative being used to support the development of both character and theme.

Style & Language

Noah's attitude, as stated in this chapter, is significant: "It would work out for him . . . it always did." The attitude is particularly revealing in regards to Noah's character development because it serves as a sign of both faith and fate—two topics that have already been established in *The Notebook* and serve to foreshadow future revelations.

Character Insight

Noah's return to what is probably his home town as well as his lack of dating since his return further develop his character. These two details demonstrate that Noah has a sense of roots and family and that he is holding on to something extremely personal and important. When the narrator tells us that Noah contemplates if he were "destined to be alone," this again refers to the idea of fate. Noah's fond remembrance of the simple sounds of the country develops Noah's character while simultaneously developing the thematic topic about what is indeed important in life.

Theme

One of the most important symbols in the novel—the Walt Whitman collection of poems called *Leaves of Grass*—is introduced in this chapter. The old book with a torn cover reveals the importance of the book for Noah. Although knowledge of this poetry collection is not essential to an understanding of *The Notebook*, it does serve as an important allusion. Readers familiar with Whitman's seminal text and its importance to the development of Whitman as an artist will gain significant insight into Noah's character.

Literary Device

The poem to which Noah refers is "A Clear Midnight," a poem that illustrates both Whitman's and Noah's tender side. The poem moves from the individual to the greater world, moving outward like a prayer. This poem is one long sentence, expressing the paradox of compression and expansion all in one. Clearly the speaker of the poem symbolizes Noah, and the apostrophe to the Soul creates a spirituality that exists within him. The Soul foreshadows the idea of soul mates—and by the end of the chapter, Allie is clearly Noah's soul mate.

The poem "A Clear Midnight" is not merely emotional, nor is it merely intellectual. But definitely, it is spiritual. The connection between the speaker of the poem and his soul mirrors the connection that Noah has—albeit yet unknown to new readers—with Allie.

From Nicholas

Noah's love for poetry, music, and the outdoors all play important roles in *The Notebook,* not only adding interest to a number of scenes but also deepening Noah as a character. How did you choose such divergent interests for this character?

A couple of the choices—his love of the outdoors and music—are, and always have been, intrinsic to the south, so those choices seemed natural. The choice to include a love of poetry, however, stemmed from my original belief that the story needed an almost lyrical aspect to the writing style to make Noah's voice come alive. Noah needed a "poetry of thought" so to speak. The movement and length of sentences and paragraphs in the final third of the novel were anything but arbitrary: I would estimate that those pages went through hundreds of variations until they finally "felt right."

Because I felt Noah's voice needed an element of poetry, I made the decision to include poetry throughout the novel. In other words, I wanted the story to feel consistent. I wanted Noah's tone and voice to make perfect sense, to feel correct, and for that, poetry needed to have been a major part of Noah's life all along.

Leaves of Grass is the poetry collection that Walt Whitman spent his entire life editing, rewriting, and adding to. Whitman was heavily influenced by transcendentalism and the romanticism that inspired it, thus indicating forms and influences of particular importance to Nicholas Sparks and *The Notebook*. Some of the elements of romanticism—the remote setting, an emphasis on emotion rather than reason, and an improbable plot—are found in *The Notebook*.

In a seemingly throw-away line early in the chapter, the narrator reveals that although Noah never married, "He had wanted to [marry] at one time." This comment also foreshadows the nature of the relationship between Noah and the unnamed lady from his past. By the end of the chapter, readers not only know her name—Allie—but they realize that Noah's ghost is no longer haunting his past; she is visiting his present.

In the flashback readers get to see Noah and Allie share their dreams—his to see the world, hers to be an artist—and this bond demonstrates that their relationship is not just physical. They are connecting as two people truly interested in the lives of one another.

Theme

Noah's neighbor, Gus, states an important theme—people work extremely hard on a particular project for one of three reasons:

1. They're crazy.

2. They're stupid.

3. They're tryin' to forget.

You can safely assume that Noah is neither crazy nor stupid, so clearly he is trying to forget someone or something. Gus' advice also can be applied to people who do not understand the actions of others. Gus' comments are another aspect of the universality of *The Notebook*.

In another seemingly throw-away line, the narrator mentions that Noah writes in his journal before going to bed at night. Not only does this develop Noah's character, but also the writing provides another bit of foreshadowing.

Readers instinctively know that Allison Nelson the 29-year-old woman is also the girl from Noah's past. The circular narration enables Sparks to build suspense, as intuitive readers recognize the particular details and are able to connect the dots before the picture is fully drawn for them. Another connection that is fully drawn but not fully identified is the similarities that Noah and Allie share. For example, both bathe at the end of the day. Water symbolizes rebirth, cleansing, and refreshing. The newspaper clipping in Allie's purse is the event that is either coincidence or fate, but regardless of which of these the reader chooses to believe, the clipping is nonetheless the spark that reconnects the separated lovers.

Character Insight

Once again, Noah is connected with poets and poetry. In fact, the narrator specifically states that "isolation . . . was good for the soul," an idea that poets understood, as did Noah. The continued comparison of Noah to a poet is the most important and sustained bit of character development in *The Notebook*. A poet is an artist and a dreamer and a person connected with nature and spirituality. And the poets with whom Noah is connected further develop his character as they reveal information about his attitudes and beliefs.

The mention of Tennyson immediately brings to mind such poems as "Break Break Break," a poem inspired by the British Romantic period and "Ulysses," a dramatic monologue from the hero of *The Odyssey* longing for something more before his death. The reference to Dylan Thomas immediately connects Noah to Thomas' most famous poem, "Do Not Go Gentle into that Good Night." The poem, a villanelle, is essentially an argument for fighting death, primarily to give closure to life by living life to the fullest until it is over. In the context of *The Notebook,* the life to which "Do Not Go Gentle" refers is the love between Noah and Allie. The poem is a symbolic imperative that commands Noah and Allie to fight for their love before they die, a command that foreshadows important events in the final chapter of *The Notebook.*

Style & Language

Nicholas Sparks transcends the form of a typical romance novel through his use of literary allusions. He develops characters and themes about the universality of the human experience of love and loss and fate and free will, rather than writes a story about reunited lovers and their hopes to rekindle past romantic flames. Although readers do not need to understand the allusions to understand the basic plot and themes of *The Notebook,* an appreciation of the seemingly insignificant references provides another layer of understanding of the sophistication of the text.

Another seemingly insignificant but actually quite important detail is how Noah refers to his beloved. To Noah, his love is "Allie" and not "Allison." This nomenclature is significant because the diminutive is a term of endearment. The importance of names is directly related to social class and social standing, which introduces the thematic topic of social inequality and the effects of social class on standing and advancement and judging others. *The Notebook* suggests that true love transcends the boundaries of time and socio-economic conditions.

Allie remembers lines from "Song of Myself," one of the poems Noah reads to her during their summer of love. "Song of Myself," one of the poems from *Leaves of Grass,* explores notions of the self and the relationship that oneself has with nature. "Song of Myself" states, paradoxically, that the self is both individual as well as universal. The poem is about sexual and spiritual union, obviously symbolizing the nature of the relationship between Noah and Allie, reiterating that their summer romance was not one of teenage lust but rather one of young adults falling deeply in love.

The chapter ends with the narrator echoing Gus' earlier sentiments that Allison is the ghost that has been haunting Noah, yet the title of the chapter is "ghosts," indicating that Noah is also a ghost for Allison.

The narrative not only switches from Allie's day to Noah's day (and back again), until the moment when their two separate stories once again combine, it also toggles between past and present, creating for the reader a sense of memory and re-memory. Sparks uses this technique to fulfill the four equally important purposes of the chapter: to provide exposition, to build suspense, to introduce the main characters, to introduce the primary conflict.

Glossary

Orion, Big Dipper, Gemini   constellations, or various groups of stars, that are identified by the shape of their grouping

Pole Star   the brightest star and handle of the Little Dipper constellation

Walt Whitman   American poet noted for his unconventional use of meter and rhyme

Leaves of Grass   a famous collection of poems by Walt Whitman

Caste system   social structure where class is determined by heredity

Tennyson   Alfred, Lord Tennyson. Famous British poet of the Victorian era

Liquidated   converted into cash

Dylan Thomas   British poet of the early modern period

Reunion

Summary

Noah and Allie stand in silence, each lost in his and her own thoughts and memories and feelings. Finally, Allie breaks the silence, greeting Noah. Awkward silence is followed by awkward, stilted conversations. Allie asks and Noah confirms that no significant other exists in his life, yet then she admits that she is not only engaged to be married, but that the wedding is in three weeks.

Noah asks all the right questions about the nature of her relationship, and Allie provides all the right answers; still Noah cannot help but wonder if Allie truly loves Lon or if she is merely trying to convince herself that she does. He then invites her to stay for a crab dinner. Allie follows Noah to the dock. While he inspects the crab cages, she inspects the dock and finds the inscription "Noah loves Allie," which was carved in the dock just days before she left, 14 years prior. Allie admires the house as Noah prepares dinner.

During their conversation, Allie reveals her mother's attitude toward social class, and Noah questions her as to why she never responded to any of his letters. Allie reveals that she never received any of them.

Allie almost admits that she felt *compelled* to come after she saw the newspaper clipping about Noah's restoration of the old house. During the course of their continued conversation, Noah is shocked to learn that Allie no longer paints; she is just as shocked to realize he not only remembered but also a painting of hers hangs in his living room.

Allie wonders if she still loves Noah. When talking about Fin and Sarah, Noah tells both Allie and readers that Fin was killed in the war. By the end of dinner, Noah is sure that he has fallen in love with the new Allie and not just the memory of the Allie of his summer love. He states that loving Allie is "his destiny."

Another new poet is mentioned—Browning. As they continue to share the evening, readers find out that Allie and Lon have never been intimate. She keeps the shirt he lent her during dinner in an effort to avoid staining her shirt. Noah asks to see her tomorrow, promising to show her a special place, and Allie agrees to meet him. She then turns away before Noah is able to attempt to kiss her.

After Allie leaves, Noah has no desire to play the guitar or to read poetry. He does not know how he feels or what he feels like doing. The chapter ends with the image of Noah crying on the porch.

Commentary

The one sentence first paragraph of this chapter effectively draws attention to the image of the long-lost lovers reunited. The lack of movement as each faces the other mirrors the idea that time has stood still.

After overcoming his initial shock and disbelief, Noah is able to begin getting reacquainted with Allie. Their sharing the chores of making dinner is an indication of domestic comfort with one another as they perform some of the necessary chores of living. During their reunion, Noah and Allie share details of their lives, filling in the gaps of their missing 14 years.

Their reunion is marred only by the inclusion of details about their forced separation. What Allie's mother believed and told Allie, that "Status is more important than feelings" and "Our future is dictated by what we are, as opposed to what we want" not only reveals much about Allie's mother, but also they serve as antithetical statements regarding important themes in *The Notebook*. Clearly, Allie's mother is an antagonist (a person who works against the protagonist and gives rise to the conflict). In this case, she not only worked to keep Noah away from Allie, but also she succeeded for 14 years.

Allie's sense of compulsion directly addresses the thematic topic of fate and destiny. Although fate may lend a hand in Allie seeing the newspaper clipping, she chose to lie to Lon and seek out Noah. Allie and Noah may have been fated to be together, but she chose to return to New Bern. She chose to visit Noah at his house. And he chose to invite her to stay.

This chapter continues the exploration of the nature of love. And rather than provide an easy-to-memorize, moral-of-the-story answer, Sparks provides examples and complications of the messiness that makes up real-world love. Clearly, love is more than a word—it encompasses the actions that accompany the words.

One of Allie's thoughts serves as an important thematic statement: "Poetry . . . wasn't written to be analyzed; it was meant to inspire without reason, to touch without understanding." This idea refers not only to poetry but also to love.

The closing image of the chapter is one of Noah alone on his porch, crying. Many critics consider this a bit of emotional blackmail, tugging on the heartstrings of the readers. Yet, realistically, what else would Noah do?

Stylistically, the closing of the chapter mirrors the beginning, ending with a single-sentence paragraph. The final sentence is commentary by the narrator, focusing on Noah's inability to control or stop his tears. Noah is overcome by his emotions and so too are most readers.

From Nicholas

***The Notebook* was your first novel made into a movie. Can you describe what that process was like? Did you, at any point, feel as though you had lost control of your story?**

The film sold to New Line Cinema in 1995; filming, however, didn't begin until 2003. There were long stretches during that period when nothing seemed to be happening, and until they actually began production, I suppose I'd come to believe that it would never be made.

The delay was caused by a multitude of factors: It took six months to find a screenwriter, who then took six months to write the screenplay. The studio, New Line Cinema, asked for a rewrite, which took another six months, but they still weren't happy. New Line then spent six months or so deciding whether or not to hire a different screenwriter. Eventually, they did, and the screenplay took about a year to get exactly right. At that point in time, rumors began to float that an extremely well known director and actor were interested in the project, so the studio waited for a year and a half to see whether they'd move on the project. It never happened. Around the same time, New Line Cinema ran into financial troubles: For a while, it was unclear whether the studio would survive. Fortunately, they took a chance on Lord of the Rings, *and the trilogy was a spectacular success. They then hired a director, who spent about six months on the project and then, for some reason, either left the project or was asked to leave. Finally, after another few months of inaction, they hired Nick Cassavetes, who loved the project. He eventually ended up directing the film and did a first-rate job.*

It's also important to realize that this circuitous was by no means extraordinary—it's more the rule than the exception. Every adaptation has its challenges, but I was fortunate that Mark Johnson, the producer, never gave up.

The purpose of this chapter is twofold: to establish the conflict and to illustrate the depths of their love. Although Noah is not involved in any personal relationship, Allie is engaged to be married. Yet, their memories and their reunion illustrates that they both have loved each other and have been in love with each other since the first summer they met, 14 years prior.

Glossary

Chasm   literally a gorge; metaphorically a gap; used here to indicate the emotional distance between Allie and others

Browning   Robert Browning, a famous British poet of the Victorian era

Phone Calls

Summary

Lon attempts to contact Allie, but he is unsuccessful. His first attempt was at 7:00 p.m., and almost three hours later, she still is not back in her hotel room. Something is bothering him, although he is unable to initially quite recall what it is. Lon remembers the rocky start their relationship had as well as the honest assessment of his life that Allie gave him after their first date. Now, four years later, he is somewhat panicked, especially when he remembers that Allie had spent a summer in the town she was going antiquing in. Her mother made fun of Allie's summer romance, but Allie had taken the romance seriously. Lon's last attempt to reach Allie is also unsuccessful.

Commentary

Lon calls from his office because staying late is standard for him, which reveals how important his career is to him, but it also offers a partial explanation for Allie's actions. If Lon puts his career ahead of his fiancé, then Allie has time to ponder her past and rethink her commitment to the relationship. Lon focuses on himself and his own needs, but his willingness to call Allie multiple times indicates that he is both concerned for her wellbeing as well as concerned about the implications this trip may have on their relationship. Although he may have been taking her for granted, Lon loves Allie.

Lon is obviously scared about what he might lose, but the more important question must be, "Is Lon more scared of losing Allie or more scared about what might happen to him?" The difference between these two extremes is immense—one focuses on Allie and the other on Lon. Readers are not currently privy to Lon's thoughts and motivations, yet the two possible interpretations of his state of mind illustrate the difference between being loved and loving another, two important thematic topics in *The Notebook*. Although this chapter is a short one, it is significant because it provides a contrast to the romantic reunion of the previous chapter as well as foreshadows the conflict yet to come.

Kayaks and Forgotten Dreams

Summary

This chapter begins by alternating the perspectives of the former lovers during the next morning. It begins with Allie, who had slept in Noah's shirt, and after a restless night, spent the early morning remembering special times from their summer together. Her thoughts turn to Noah and the present, wondering if he too was enjoying the coming of dawn.

And he is. Noah wakes early and takes a kayak up the river, allowing his time on the river to refresh both his body and his mind. He spends most of his time on the river contemplating why Allie had come to visit him. Noah returns home after spending two hours on the river, chops wood, and gets ready for Allie's arrival.

Switching back to Allie, the narration returns to her morning. She spends her time wandering downtown and thinking about Lon. She finds an art gallery, though she is unimpressed with most of the work. After leaving the gallery, she goes to a department store to purchase some art supplies—paper, chalk, and pencils—and spends the remainder of the morning rediscovering her talent. On her way out of the hotel, the manager stops Allie to tell her that Lon had called four times the previous evening. Allie is momentarily concerned about the importance of the repeated calls but rationalizes that she cannot reach him now because he is in court and leaves to meet Noah, entirely dismissing the missed calls, and not knowing or caring that two minutes after she leaves Lon attempts once again to reach her.

Commentary

The morning parallels their innate connection—both spend time doing something they love and are somewhat pleasantly surprised to find they had spent two hours doing it. This indicates the old cliché that "time flies when you're having fun." It also indicates the maturity of the relationship, for both Allie and Noah are doing things independently of one another, indicating that their relationship is not co-dependent but rather co-enriching.

Literary Device

The mention of forthcoming rain literally refers to the incoming weather pattern. But the rain also has metaphorical significance. The wonderful reunion that Noah and Allie are having is akin to a bright, sunny day; however, before they know it and sooner than they could imagine, the heavens are going to open up, and into their reunion a major rain storm is going to take place.

Allie considers the possibility that Lon found out the truth about her trip, but she immediately dismisses that idea—which is incorrect—and she also thinks she cannot contact him because he is in court, which is also incorrect. Both of these incorrect assumptions illustrate that she is not as connected with Lon as much as she would like to be.

Not only does Allie lie to the manager, but also she instructs him to lie to Lon, if indeed Lon even were to call. This instance is the second time that Allie has been untruthful to her fiancé, which is further indication that everything in their relationship is not as idealistic as she would like or need it to be.

Glossary

Elayn perhaps a reference to artist Elayn Kuehler, a Romantic Realist, or perhaps an amalgam of artists

Moving Water

Summary

Allie arrives around noon and greets Noah with a kiss on the cheek. Eager for the surprise, Allie immediately demands to know where it is. Noah tells her that it is about a mile up the river but is concerned that with the impending rain she might get wet. Undaunted, Allie decides to risk getting wet in order to see the someplace special.

While canoeing to the special place, Allie asks Noah what he most remembers from their summer together, and he replies "All of it." His explanation reveals that he is not being coy but rather that summer had such a profound impact on his life that there is no way to possibly favor one aspect over another. Allie is stunned and moved by the sincerity and depth of Noah's reply. She compares the relationship she has with Lon, realizing that she does love her fiancé, just not the same way that she loves Noah.

Commentary

Literary
Device

The significance of the chapter title is that the words have both literal and metaphorical interpretations. The literal moving water refers to the creek water and the falling rain. The metaphorical water is the renewal of their relationship, water symbolizing rebirth, new life, and a cleansing. The rain also foreshadows the storm their relationship is going to face.

When explaining his answer to Allie's question about his summer memories, Noah describes love "as an emotion that we can't control, one that overwhelms logic and common sense." For him, this describes both their summer of love and the nature of their relationship.

Character
Insight

The mentioning of T.S. Eliot reveals yet another side of Noah's character. As a poet, Eliot is more abstract and intellectual than Whitman. Eliot's most famous poem is the epic *The Waste Land,* which could be a veiled reference to the state of Noah's emotional well being. An important aspect of Noah and Allie's relationship is made clear when readers learn that Lon did not understand Allie's abstract painting. Lon clearly does not understand the depths of Allie's passion and soul, whereas, Noah encourages Allie to develop her own gifts and passions. This demonstrates that Noah has a connection with and an understanding of Allie as a person and an artist, a connection and understanding that is currently missing in Allie's life.

The chapter ends with suspense and anticipation: What is it that Noah wants to show Allie? And what effect will it have on their reunion?

Glossary

Osprey   a large hawk, also known as a fish hawk

Mullet   a cylindrical, gray fish, also known as a goatfish

Swans and Storms

Summary

Noah's surprise is a small lake that is filled with Tundra swan and Canada geese. They sit in silence for a while, admiring the beauty and splendor of nature. Allie feeds some of them bread, and the moment is only ended by the sound of thunder in the distance. Although Noah paddles quickly, they are unable to beat the rain back to Noah's house, and by the time they arrive, they are soaked. Allie puts on some of Noah's clothes.

Allie watches Noah stoke the fire. They share a drink in front of the warmth, rekindling the logs as well as their love. Noah admits to Allie that she was his first love as well as his first lover. Allie admits that she wrote Noah letters but never mailed them. Noah then admits to Allie that he loves her—not the memory of her but the Allie of here and now. After his profession of love, Allie tells Noah that she has never physically been with another man. After a few more memories, they succumb to their passion, to their love. Noah and Allie spend the day together, making love, and rediscovering each other all over again.

Commentary

The title of the chapter is a juxtaposition of beauty and violence. A swan is also highly symbolic. Often swans are associated with divine inspiration, as well as beauty and creativity. According to legend, swans also mate for life. The committed love that Noah has had for Allie as well as Allie's lack of sexual intimacy with another man indicate that they have both, in a sense, mated for life with one another.

Although storms are violently powerful, Allie claims they have always seemed "romantic" to her. This comment is the closest readers have seen Allie wanting to initiate and act on the romantic relationship she previously had with Noah. The previous night, she was unwilling and unable to allow Noah to even attempt a kiss goodnight. Now, after an honest sharing of emotions, she is both willing and able to re-consummate their relationship. The emotional connection precedes the physical, which is important for it demonstrates that this feeling is not just a sexual attraction and sexual compatibility that two have. The sex scenes are neither graphic nor gratuitous; rather, they are truly the description of a couple making love, expressing physically the deep emotional and spiritual connection that they share. Fourteen years ago, when they were saying their goodbyes, Noah slipped Allie a note containing the words, "our souls are connected." He also mentioned finding each other again. At the time, neither of them could have imagined a reunion as perfect as this.

Literary Device

While they are discussing their past, Noah simply states, "I wish you could have read the letters I wrote you." This line is not only a realistic part of their dialogue, but also it is a bit of foreshadowing. And the penultimate paragraph of the chapter not only foreshadows the rest of the book, it contains Noah's profession of love, one of the most direct statements of feelings in *The Notebook.*

Theme

Noah tells Allie, "You are the answer to every prayer I've offered . . . I don't know how I could have lived without you for as long as I have. I love you, Allie . . . I always have, and I always will." These lines connect the thematic topics of religion, faith, fate, free will, and spirituality, leaving both Allie and readers speechless.

Glossary

Bourbon   whiskey distilled from a mash of primarily corn but also malt, and rye

Courtrooms

Summary

Lon makes an unusual request to suspend the current trial until Monday. His request is agreed on by opposing counsel, and reluctantly the judge grants it. After receiving the postponement, Lon leaves for New Bern.

Commentary

This chapter is the shortest in the novel, and the pace of the chapter matches the brevity of its length. Lon's shaking hands indicate his nervousness and apprehension; they are a physical representation of his fear of the unknown. But, by leaving a trial for the first time, Lon is demonstrating his love for Allie as well as his fear of losing her. Finally, he is putting his relationship ahead of his career.

In addition to developing the character of Lon, this chapter is needed for the conflict of the main story line—although Allie loves the moment she is currently sharing with Noah, she needs to see Lon and figure out in person what she is going to do. Like the cliché statement, Lon is currently "out of sight, out of mind." But when he is back in sight, in person, Allie faces a much tougher decision. She is caught up in the moment of love and passion and romance, but she also has to take a logical look at the status of her life and make a well-thought-out assessment as to what will really make her happy and what is truly the right thing to do.

An Unexpected Visitor

Summary

After spending the night together, Noah and Allie also share the next morning. The morning is spent eating breakfast, making love, doing chores, talking, and even staring at one another. After lunch there is knock on the door, and Noah is shocked to see Allie's mother, Anne.

Allie's mother says "I came because I had to"—the same reason she assumes that Allie came to New Bern. Allie's mother reveals that Lon called her last night to ask about Noah and tells Allie that he is also on his way to New Bern. In addition, Anne delivers Noah's letters, which she has never read, to Allie. After Allie and her mother share statements of love for one another, Anne departs.

Commentary

Based on the title of the chapter, readers are expecting the confrontation between Allie and Lon; however, that is momentarily on hold as the lovers must first confront the person who actively worked to keep them apart.

Character Insight

While explaining why she has come, Anne treats Allie as an adult and a friend and not as a child. This moment is important, for otherwise Anne would be a stereotypical, stuck up, Southern aristocrat. Rather than make excuses for her actions, Anne attempts to explain that she thought she was protecting her daughter from an unsuitable match. When Anne asks Allie if she should stay in town, she is offering what help and assistance Allie may want or need while simultaneously giving her daughter the space, room, and support she needs to make this very important decision. The ambiguous ending to the chapter, the uncertainty of Allie hearing her mother whispering "Follow your heart" may just be Allie's projection of what she wanted her mother to say, or it may be her mother's attempt at atoning for the mistakes of her past.

The shorter chapters—this one and the previous one—increase the pace and suspense of the narrative, contrasting with the leisurely pace of the time Allie and Noah spend together alone. When they are by themselves, Noah and Allie are lost in time, but when others are around and involved, they are cognizant of their surroundings and are caught up in the hustle and bustle of real-world life.

Crossroads

Summary

After Anne leaves, Allie is torn, claiming to want "a happy ending without hurting anyone." Not wanting to lose her again, Noah asks Allie to stay with him. Though she wants to stay with Noah, Allie is not sure she can. Allie gives Noah the sketch she drew earlier in the morning, a sketch composed of Noah's face and the current state of his house. They embrace and kiss and admit their love for one another. Noah watches Allie drive off, believing that she is driving out of his life forever. And as she exits, he likens Allie to her mother—remarking that both women make decisions and then never look back.

Commentary

Literary
Device

The significance of this title is both metaphorical and symbolic—in their lives and in their relationship. They truly are at a vital intersection where important decisions need to be made. Noah recognizes that they are adults and can't live their lives for others; Allie is torn between the life she was making and the life she wants to have with Noah. She does love both men in her life, just differently.

Not revealing the subject of the sketch that Allie was working on for two hours in the morning until after Allie collects her belongings suggests finality in their relationship. The sketch—a current likeness of Noah and the current state of his remodeled house—captures the reunion and simultaneously serves as a goodbye gift, something by which Noah can remember her and the past 48 hours.

A Letter from Yesterday

Summary

Allie gets her crying under control as she drives back to the inn, and by the time she arrives she notices that Lon's car is parked in the lot. Instead of getting out and going to Lon, Allie reaches for the stack of unread letters from Noah. And instead of reading the first one, Allie decides to read the last one, the goodbye letter. Noah's letter was a heartfelt statement of love that expressed the finality of their situation without diluting or sacrificing the significance of their summer together. Noah wrote about the nature of their love and the fond memories that he will always cherish. Allie reads the letter three times before she gets up the courage to go and speak to Lon.

Commentary

This chapter ends the inner story of the frame narrative. It leaves readers in suspense, for they do not know if Allie is either getting her courage up to break up with Lon or using Noah's own words against him as a means for her to again walk away.

This chapter is another short one that Sparks uses to build suspense. There are also two paragraphs that consist of only a single sentence each. These sentences, along with the contents of Noah's final letter to Allie, create a mood of finality. Sparks also creates a sense of distance between readers and the situation by having almost half of the paragraphs starting with the word "she." Using a pronoun instead of Allie's name is a technique that depersonalizes the character. As a character, Allie is moving away from the reader as she literally and metaphorically moves away from Noah.

Ironically, as the narrator tells the reader that Allie remains uncertain of her decision until she sees Lon in the lobby, it is that exact image that makes readers uncertain of Allie's decision. Not being privy to Allie's thoughts at this time, readers are left with the same uncertainty that Noah is simultaneously experiencing. At the end of the previous chapter, Noah thinks about how much Allie and her mother have in common, and a similar thought crosses the mind of readers, cannot be certain exactly whom Allie is going to choose. Emotionally, readers are rooting for Noah, but intellectually, they are not sure if Allie walks away from him because it may be the easier choice to make.

Winter for Two

Summary

The narrative returns to the original, outer frame story, and the unnamed narrator closes the notebook. The narrator admits that he is going to reveal some of his secrets. First of all, he reveals that he has been married for almost 49 years, and although he is not supposed to see his wife at night, he sometimes breaks this rule.

The narrator knows that the woman he is reading to is dying, though she does not. As the narrator talks about his experiences, he quotes from a poem. Then he talks about visiting and reading to other residents.

After finishing reading from the notebook, he takes his wife's hand; she asks if he wrote the story and he admits he did. She asks which one did she marry, and he replies that she will know by the end of the day. He is convinced this day is going to be a good day. His wife does not know who he is, and thus she asks him, "Who are you?"

From Nicholas

The structure of *The Notebook* is unique: It begins and ends in the present day, spends the majority of the story in 1946, and flashes back to 1932 and the years in between. Why did you decide to tell it this way, instead of chronologically?

Pacing, structure, chronology and timelines are tools; if effectively used by an author, they aid in generating authentic emotional power. While the analogy might not be perfect, try to think of those tools as musical notes. It's possible to arrange those notes in an obvious pattern (low pitch to high pitch) for example. The resulting tones might even be lovely. Yet, by varying the pattern, the music might resonate more deeply. The same rules apply in writing.

In this case, I employed structure and chronology to move the reader through the story in such a way as to allow the reader to identify strongly with Noah, especially toward the end. The love Noah felt for Allie felt real to the reader, and consequently, so did Noah's heartbreak.

Before he answers, the narrative flashes back, explaining that they have lived here for three years. The reader learns that the narrator has arthritis, which prevents him from holding his wife's hands with their fingers interlocked, and this is sad for him.

Returning to the present, readers now know for almost certainty that the narrator is Noah, for he refers to his daddy, yet he tells his wife that his name is Duke, and he tells her that her name is Hannah. Because of previous slips of the tongue, Noah has hurt Allie during their time here, and Noah is determined not to do that again, and thus, he lies.

Again Noah quotes from another unidentified poem, although he does identify the poet as Whitman. After this, Noah provides an overview of his married life with Allie, mentioning that she became a famous artist. In the present, Noah now spends his time wooing Allie, slowly and gently.

He then quotes a line from Sir Charles Sedley. After that, he talks about Allie's last year before moving to the extended care facility, after she was diagnosed with the beginning stages of Alzheimer's. Noah shares some of the letters Allie wrote to him and that he wrote to her.

In Noah's final letter, he recounts telling their children about the decision Allie had to make and that is how readers find out about her decision to stay with the one man she has always loved.

From Nicholas

Allie's fiancé is a good man, who loves her, earns a fine living, and is considered a good catch in her circle. Yet with Noah, Allie shares an indescribable passion. Do you believe readers respond to this novel because of that passion, because of the difficult choice between financial security and social acceptance on the one hand and passionate love on the other?

Of course. In life, we have to make choices, and often the hardest are those that ask us to choose between what our heart wants and what the mind thinks is best. It's universal and inevitable, which is why the choice rings so true. For the reader, the beauty of her final decision lies in the fact that Allie's passionate choice ended up being the right choice.

In Noah's final letter to Allie, he writes, "I am who I am because of you."

Noah compares the progression of Allie's Alzheimer's to other patients who are at the home; he admits that mornings are extremely difficult for her, and she cries inconsolably; Allie also sees gnomes.

Some days, after Noah reads to her, Allie's condition improves, and she wants to remember the day that he spends with her. On her good days, they eat dinner together in Allie's room. This time, at the window, Allie concludes that the woman in the story chooses Noah. She then remembers and calls him Noah. And then she gets frightened of losing this memory and these feelings, but Noah responds, "What we have is forever."

But the moment is ruined when Allie sees the gnomes.

The nurses come in response to Noah's hitting the button, and eight days after Noah's good day with Allie, he suffers a stroke. Noah spends some days in and out of consciousness and partially recovers, but he has right side paralysis. After Noah is released from the hospital, he returns to the home, and in an evening of loneliness he reads the last letter Allie wrote to him. She mentions her return after breaking her engagement to Lon; through her letter, readers find out that Allie is the one who commanded Noah to write their story down and read it to her.

After reading the letter, Noah decides to go to Allie's room, even though it is against the rules.

From Nicholas

For Noah, having truly loved is the hallmark of his life; it is what gives his life meaning. Do you believe that everyone, no matter what else they may achieve, yearns to experience this sort of love?

The desire to be loved unconditionally is nearly universal and at first glance, that seems to be the subject of the novel. The true theme, however, is just the opposite. The Notebook (as told from Noah's perspective) actually explores the beauty and power of loving, as opposed to being loved. Framing the story in this way suggests that love is a gift, one that not only benefits the one who's loved, but also the one who loves as well.

Nurse Janice commands him not to go to Allie's room, even though it is their 49th wedding anniversary, but she then tells him that she needs to fill her coffee. Noah feels entirely alone in the world until he notices that her coffee cup is full, so he slowly enters Allie's room. He has a note to place under her pillow. After approaching Allie, Noah kisses her on the mouth, and she mentions his name and begins to unbutton his shirt. Noah claims they both are beginning "to slip toward heaven" as the novel closes.

Commentary

This last chapter is the longest chapter of the novel. This length emphasizes the importance of the events in this chapter. And although the chapter begins with "the story ends there," clearly it does not.

The first untitled poem excerpt is from John Clare's "First Love." The speaker of this poem begins by being in a state of physical shock and emotional distress and ends with a desire for self-knowledge about a vision of his beloved. And a poem that is often an intertext with "First Love" is Byron's "She Walks in Beauty." Clearly, the speakers in both of these poems represent Noah, and the two women symbolize Allie. Allie was Noah's "first love," and they both are currently in a state of physical and emotional distress. And Noah longs to have his miracle good days when he can see his beloved once again. "She Walks in Beauty" is about a woman's beauty, both physical and spiritual, and that is the essence of the beauty that Noah sees and adores in Allie.

The second excerpt is from Walt Whitman's "To a Common Prostitute." Initially, this passage may seem like an odd choice to include in a novel about love relationships, but reading the poem reveals two important components: the seemingly obvious interpretation of the poem, the assertion that "prostitutes are people, too" is a request to respect all life—whether it is the life of a prostitute or the life of a person suffering from Alzheimer's. Yet another level equates the act of prostitution to the act of writing poetry. If Allie is the symbolic prostitute and Noah is the poet, then their physical union is itself a poetical expression. And the dedication and commitment that Noah is demonstrating to and for Allie by reading to her daily is a type of poetry in motion, a gesture that does a lot of good for both partners.

Character Insight

The Whitman excerpt is followed by Noah's admission that he reads in order to "know who I am." This is a clear indication that an analysis of the poems will aid in an understanding of Noah and Allie. He is a poet. A man in search of himself. A man longing to see his one true love again (in her moments of mental clarity). And a man who is willing to wait patiently and sacrifice selflessly for the woman he loves.

Literary Device

An analysis of the next quoted poem makes Noah's character abundantly clear. Although it is not identified by name or by poet, Walt Whitman's "The Sleepers," another selection from *Leaves of Grass,* is quoted. And not only does it provide insight into the nature of Noah and Allie's relationship, it foreshadows the ending of *The Notebook.*

The dominant symbolism of "The Sleepers" is night, which is a rather common symbol for death; sleep implies death and, at the same time, the release of the soul through death. The poet identifies himself as merging with other beings and multitudes of beings and thus establishes a spiritual and psychological kinship with them. The poet's vision or dream motif is the core of the structure and the apparent lack of organization reflects the quality of the dream itself.

Literary Device

Thus the poem's structure, theme, and symbolism are brought into a cohesive and meaningful pattern, just as Sparks achieves in *The Notebook.* Throughout "The Sleepers" men and women become beautiful in sleep. Beauty, associated with darkness, attains a spiritual quality which is the essential element in the poet's mystical experience. The structure, themes, and symbolism of *The Notebook* all address a need and desire for beautiful, mystical, love experiences.

It is extremely significant that Noah lies to Allie and says his name is Duke and hers is Hannah. Many people believe that perception is reality. And Noah needs Allie to be as calm as possible. He knows that reading to her sometimes—not often but sometimes—enables her to remember who she is, who he is, and remember their life together. But those times are few and far between. And because Noah is not initially certain whether she is going to have a good day, a miracle, he plays the part of a man who loves and cares for her, even if he cannot tell her his real name. This illustrates an interesting concept—that actions are neither right nor wrong—they merely are, and it is the context in which an action takes place determines the appropriateness or inappropriateness of it. Noah's lie to Allie is a lie told out of love and respect and thus cannot be considered wrong.

The next poem that is mentioned by author but not by title is "Continuities" by Walt Whitman. This poem, also included in Whitman's *Leaves of Grass,* seems to explicitly address Allie's Alzheimer's, especially the line "appearance must not foil, nor shifted sphere confuse thy brain." Noah simultaneously reassures Allies, readers, and himself that the little white lie he is telling is not problematic, for the sense of resurrection and rebirth mentioned in the poem symbolize the occasional good days that Allie has. And those few good days are enough to survive the difficult other days.

The next poem that Noah recites to Allie is credited solely to a "wise poet," and that poet is non-other than Nicholas Sparks, illustrating that he has success as a poet as well as a novelist. In fact, the final three poems cited in *The Notebook* are actually written by Sparks himself. And it is this combination of roles that is responsible Noah's next insightful observation. Noah compares his relationship with Allie to dusk, the time of day when day becomes night. He states that "there cannot be one without the other, yet they cannot exist at the same time . . . always together, forever apart." This is the struggle Noah has reading daily to Allie, not knowing if that day will be a miracle day or not. Noah recounts that he first wrote this to Allie in the last letter he wrote to her, and she was reading it at twilight. That same later reveals how the love that Noah and Allie shared together lead to being incredible parents to their children, as Noah revealed to his adult children (in addition to readers) the story of Allie's goodbye to Lon and the difficulty she and he both had saying goodbye to one another. Noah's statement, "I am who I am because of you," takes into account their first summer, their years apart, as well as their years together.

It is rather coy that Noah constantly mentions and recites lines of poetry. Many critics see these references as indirect critiques of Lon's question regarding Allie's painting, asking her what it was supposed to be, when it was an abstract painting whose purpose was to elicit thought. The lines of quoted poetry fit specifically to the plot of *The Notebook* at the time they are being used. However, they provide a deeper understanding of character and thematic development when readers understand the original source material.

Two important statements in this chapter serve as direct statements of theme for *The Notebook.* The first is when Noah says that "life is simply a collection of little lives, each lived one day at a time. That each day should be spent finding beauty in flowers and poetry and talking to animals." The second is "a day spent with dreaming and sunsets and refreshing breezes cannot be bettered" for life exists "for falling in love." The use of polysyndeton (the deliberate use of unnecessary conjunctions) slows down the rhythm of the sentence in order to emphasize the little things in daily life that are actually important in living a meaningful life. The syntax of the sentence parallels the message of the statement—to slow down, live one day at a time while making the most out of that day. Enjoy nature. Appreciate one another. Fall in love. These commands are seemingly simple but extremely difficult to follow.

Theme

Another important thematic statement from this chapter is "Romance and passion are possible at any age." This speaks to the importance of maintaining relationships, especially as we age. Young adults do not have a monopoly on romance. Successful love relationships are the result of hard work, dedication, and commitment. Yet, we are never too old to stop romancing and wooing our loved ones, for everyone wants to feel special and needs to feel special. Loving another is more important than being loved.

The narrative of *The Notebook* then takes the reader through the exact experience that Noah has—just as readers are enjoying the reunion between Allie and Noah, for her mind and memories have returned, and Allie and Noah experience a day of being in love with one another, and it is a reunion for readers, too. Readers already have experienced the beautiful love relationship once and enjoy being a part of another miracle. Yet, as quickly as Noah and Allie are reunited, it is taken away—from them and from the readers. Instead of an ideal reunion, readers experience the image of two people who need consoling—"A woman shaking in fear from demons in her own mind, and the old man who loves her more deeply than life itself, crying softly in the corner." This powerful scene evokes empathy for Noah in all readers, as we feel the anguish he feels, and we understand why Noah feels so alone.

Character Insight

Not only does Noah spend the rest of the day alone in his room, but also he introduces the reader to another character who is alone—Dr. Barnwell. The doctor's desire to be completely devoted to career and family is situation that parallels Noah's, and Noah realizes this as he tells Dr. Barnwell that both of them are alone. Dr. Barnwell represents all people—like Lon—who put their career or something else ahead of the people they love. Ironically, it is Dr. Barnwell who tells Noah that "no one is alone," for he does not realize the contradiction that he himself is living, and although Noah attempts to explain the harsh reality to him, Noah is unable to get through to the doctor.

After the miracle day, Noah is begrudgingly optimistic, realizing that the four hours he had with Allie were indeed a miracle, a gift from God, and he slowly returns to his typical routine. He mentions that he finds a "Strange comfort in the predictability of my life." This indicates the importance of regularity and continuity.

Literary Device

One of the predictable things in Noah's life is the creek that he can see outside the window of his room. It regularly rises and falls with the rain. The constant ebbing and flowing of the waters symbolize Noah's life, and Noah articulates this.

After Noah's stroke, readers are able to read a letter from Allie to Noah. In it, readers find out that after Allie left to see Lon, when she returned, Noah welcomed her back with a smile and an offer of a cup of coffee. And he never brought up the incident again. Allie's letter to Noah is a love letter that shows remarkable insight about the progression of her disease. It is incredibly perceptive and loving to share the knowledge that you will be losing the memory of the one you love the most and preparing him for that day. Allie is being proactive, recognizing her own loss of recognition of Noah as well as the having the insight to say "I love you" and explain to him that she does love him, even if she can't say it. Allie knows that Noah will keep the letter to reread on especially difficult days, which, of course, is exactly what he is doing.

The writing in Allie's letter is pure poetry, just like the poetry that Noah puts under Allie's pillow. And the poetry this time is Nicholas Sparks' own writing—again not only demonstrating his artistry but also demonstrating the love Sparks has for his own wife. Of course, all the letters that Noah writes to Allie and that Allie writes to him are Sparks' own writings, too, which further illustrates the deep connection and love relationship he has with Cathy.

By now, readers realize that the miracles mentioned in the opening chapter of *The Notebook* refer to the miracle of a long-lasting, committed love relationship as well as the miracle of recognition. The final reference to heaven serves as a metaphor on a variety of levels—it is the state of Noah's mind as he is in the arms of his beloved wife; it is a metaphor for sexual ecstasy; and it is a metaphor for both death and the reward for the two who die in each other's arms.

Note: The ambiguous nature of the ending of *The Notebook* is not nearly so ambiguous if readers take Sparks' sequel *The Wedding* into consideration. Noah, a character in this novel, is alive and well and believes that Allie has been reincarnated as a swan.

Glossary

Everglades   a swampy yet partially forested region in southern Florida

Vanna's   a reference to Vanna White, the hostess for the TV game show *Wheel of Fortune*

Eliot   T.S. Eliot. Famous British poet of the modern era

John Wayne   famous American actor, star of westerns, known as "Duke"

Alzheimer's   a progressive form of dementia that begins with gradual memory loss and eventually leads to complete helplessness

Gnomes   fabled race of dwarflike creatures

Mozart   Amadeus Mozart, famous and prolific Austrian composer

CHARACTER ANALYSES

The following character analyses delve into the physical, emotional, and psychological traits of the literary work's major characters so that you might better understand what motivates these characters. The writer of this study guide provides this scholarship as an educational tool by which you may compare your own interpretations of the characters. Before reading the character analyses that follow, consider first writing your own short essays on the characters as an exercise by which you can test your understanding of the original literary work. Then, compare your essays to those that follow, noting discrepancies between the two. If your essays appear lacking, that might indicate that you need to re-read the original literary work or re-familiarize yourself with the major characters.

Noah

Noah is the main character (protagonist) of *The Notebook*. He is the hero. Noah represents true love, true faith, and true artistry. In one sense, *The Notebook* is similar to a medieval morality play, and Noah is a contemporary "Everyman." The characters in a morality play were symbolic representations used to illustrate an idea; Noah represents true, faithful, committed love. Noah remains true to Allie even when he does not know if he will ever even see her again.

In many regards, Noah is the ideal man—he is faithful, idealistic, strong, good looking, a poet, and helpful to those in need. The Noah of the main narrative is almost too good to be true. He has a strong relationship with family and friends and is respectful to both nature and authority. He seemingly has no faults.

The Noah of the frame story is older yet still exhibits the same characteristics; he is also loyal, faithful, committed, strong, and realistic. The dedication he demonstrates to both his wife and the other residents of the extended care facility is utterly amazing.

Finally, Noah can be seen as a symbol for Nicholas Sparks himself, and *The Notebook,* which is dedicated to his wife, who is his best friend, is Sparks' own love story. The story inspired by Cathy's grandparents is one long love letter from the man who truly seems to be practicing what he preaches.

Allie

Allie wants the best of both worlds as she represents the different types of love that exist. In essence she is the embodiment of a thematic topic. As Allie grows and matures, so does her understanding of love. Her growth symbolizes the development of real love—from a potential summer fling through a tough decision to a career-creating relationship that yields children who are the product of that committed love.

Her relationship with Noah reveals the essence of true love—where one is able to develop one's own talents, skills, and abilities. Allie is able to develop as an artist, and a character, because of Noah's love for her. Yet, she is not dependent solely on Noah, for she makes important decisions—she chooses to seek him out, she chooses him over Lon, and she chooses to write an emotional an insightful letter to Noah in order help him deal with her illness.

Lon

Lon is the stereotypical, self-obsessed individual who realizes too late that his self-absorption is going to cost him his fiancée. Lon is also the embodiment of the conflict in *The Notebook.* As a character, he is the one readers know as the obstacle to Allie's love. He is a dynamic character, but his change is a little too late.

Anne

Anne is the antagonist. Although she works to keep Noah and Allie apart, she cannot be considered a villain, for she is not evil. Anne represents the difficulties that many parents have when trying to steer their children to adulthood. Fourteen years later, she attempts to atone for earlier mistakes, first by preparing Allie for Lon's impending visit, then by offering her support without being pushy. She also finally gives Noah's letters to Allie, and her final words may be encouraging Allie to follow her heart.

CRITICAL
ESSAYS

On the pages that follow, the writer of this study guide provides critical scholarship on various aspects of Nicholas Sparks' *The Notebook*. These interpretive essays are intended solely to enhance your understanding of the original literary work; they are supplemental materials and are not to replace your reading of *The Notebook*. When you're finished reading *The Notebook,* and prior to your reading this study guide's critical essays, consider making a bulleted list of what you think are the most important themes and symbols. Write a short paragraph under each bullet explaining *why* you think that theme or symbol is important; include at least one short quote from the original literary work that supports your contention. Then, test your list and reasons against those found in the following essays. Do you include themes and symbols that the study guide author doesn't? If so, this self test might indicate that you are well on your way to understanding original literary work. But if not, perhaps you will need to re-read *The Notebook*.

Narrative Techniques: Sparks' Literary Form

Instead of starting at the beginning and telling the story in chronological order, Nicholas Sparks begins *The Notebook* near the end of what would be a linear narration and then employs both the framing technique and flashback to tell his tale.

The main storyline is the reunion of Noah and Allie and the conflict that they face as they must decide the path their lives will now take. This particular event only lasts three days in 1946; however, important information that shapes their reunion occurred weeks and years earlier. If you imagine a picture in a frame, the reunion is the photograph. And the opening and closing chapters of the novel are set in the present, some 49 years later. The present-day storyline frames the reunion story. Although the frame represents the present and current storyline and the picture represents the reunion, within these two main storylines are other stories, some are episodes and others are vignettes, which are told in the form of a flashback. These stories, told within the context of the other storylines, fit within both the picture and the frame. And some of these smaller stories of earlier events frame even smaller stories of other events. Each story is distinct within itself while simultaneously being an integral part of a greater whole; every individual picture is a part of a bigger picture.

This framework technique provides the structure of the plot, and flashback is the technique Sparks uses to tell the stories. Characters reveal these "framed" stories through their shared and private memories. Often the reader shares a flashback with a character that is not shared with any other character.

The narrator also provides information. The narrator of *The Notebook* in the opening and closing chapters is Noah. But the narrator of the middle chapters provides a limited, third-person omniscient point of view. This perspective sometimes allows the readers into the mind of a character—typically Noah and Allie—but sometimes does not—such as Anne and Lon. This technique is important because it allows the storyline to flow seamlessly from past to present and back again.

Stylistically, the narrative techniques work well because *The Notebook* is not just a love story; the novel also explores the nature of fate and free will and the way people interact with one another. The intricacies of relationships parallel the intricacies of poetry and the framing technique enables Sparks to weave the past together with the present, leading to the emotional climax and creating a compelling read along the way.

Fate versus Free Will

Are people truly responsible for their actions? This question has puzzled humanity throughout history. Over the centuries, people have pondered the influence of divine or diabolical power, environment, genetics, even entertainment, as determining how free any individual is in making moral choices. The ancient Greeks acknowledged the role of Fate as a reality outside the individual that shaped and determined human life. In modern times, the concept of fate has developed the misty halo of romantic destiny, which is how fate is viewed in *The Notebook.*

After spending just one summer together and then not being able to contact one another for fourteen years, the article spotting could be coincidence. Or it could be fate. Regardless of how that specific incident is viewed, Allie still has the power to act on her knowledge and feelings. She chooses to seek out Noah. She chooses to spend the evening and the next day (and the next night) with him. And she chooses to break off her engagement with Lon. The reader cannot know, nor speculate, the events that do not transpire outside the pages of *The Notebook,* but you can analyze what does occur.

Noah does agree to visit with Allie. Noah does invite her to spend the next day with him. And Noah does profess his love to her. Still, Allie chooses to leave Noah and face Lon before making any decisions. It is utterly romantic to believe that Noah and Allie are fated to be together, and that is the thematic essence of *The Notebook.* Nicholas Sparks, in an interview, stated that as an author, he is "addressing different aspects of love: everlasting love, first love, and second chances at love." These are important themes in all of his novels, and these themes "provide the subtext of the novel in addition to providing the unwritten subtext of the novel that the reader experiences. The subtext—what the author endeavors to show without explanation—gives the novel deeper meaning." Thus, the complex relationship between fate and free will is mirrored in the complex relationship between different aspects of love.

CliffsNotes Review

Use this CliffsNotes Review to test your understanding of the original text, and reinforce what you have learned in this book. After you work through the review and essay questions, identify the quote section, and the fun and useful practice projects, you are well on your way to understanding a comprehensive and meaningful interpretation of *The Notebook*.

Q&A

1. What is the name of Noah's hometown?

   a. Winston Salem

   b. New Bern

   c. Ashville

2. With which poet is Noah primarily associated?

   a. Emily Dickenson

   b. Ralph Waldo Emerson

   c. Walt Whitman

3. Noah shows Allie which animals?

   a. A doe and her fawn

   b. Swan and geese

   c. Bunnies and chicks

4. What is the subject of the sketch Allie draws for Noah after their reunion?

   a. A contemporary Noah and his house

   b. An older Noah with his house

   c. Clementine on the dock

5. Why is it so important for Noah to visit Allie on the final evening in the novel?

   a. It is Allie's birthday.

   b. It is Noah's birthday.

   c. It is Noah and Allie's anniversary.

Answers: (1) b. (2) c. (3) b. (4) a. (5) c.

Identify the Quote: Find Each Quote in *The Notebook*

1. "A person can get used to anything, if given enough time."

2. "Poetry wasn't written to be analyzed; it was meant to inspire without reason, to touch without understanding."

3. "Follow your heart."

4. "You can't live your life for other people. You've got to do what's right for you, even if it hurts some people you love."

5. "For at that moment, the world is full of wonder as I feel her fingers reach for the buttons on my shirt and slowly, ever so slowly, she begins to undo them one by one."

Answers: (1) Noah, as an older man in the opening chapter commenting upon his daily routine and the daily routine of all the residents of Creekside. (2) Allie, thinks this after her reunion with Noah, as they are sitting in the dark on Noah's porch. (3) Anne, Allie thinks she hears her mother whisper these words as Anne exits Noah's house. (4) Noah, as he attempts to convince Allie to stay with him instead of going back to Lon. (5) Noah, as he is visiting Allie at night. This is the last line of the novel.

Review Questions and Essay Topics

1. Note the role of Gus in the second chapter ("Ghosts"). How is his role important? What key information does he provide? What statements provide thematic commentary and which foreshadow future events? Make a list of the other minor characters. What important roles do other minor characters play in *The Notebook*? Be sure to consider how they develop the characters, plot, and theme of *The Notebook*.

2. Is any character in *The Notebook* truly a villain? Is there a bad guy? Differentiate between an antagonist and a villain. If no villain exists, how do you explain the difficulties that Noah and Allie endure? How does the lack of a clear-cut villain support the development of characters, plot, and themes?

3. Compare and contrast the relationship that Noah has with his father to the one that Allie has with her mother. What is the significance of this juxtaposition? How do the relationships Noah and Allie have with their parents significant to the relationships they have with their own children? What is the thematic significance of this?

4. Identify the different settings in *The Notebook* and analyze their significance for developing character, plot, and theme. Pay particular attention to areas of isolation and how characters share their personal isolated areas with others.

5. Are Noah and Allie more accurately categorized as fully developed *characters* or *caricatures*? Are the realistic elements of *The Notebook* believable? Which parts, if any, push the limits of reality?

Practice Projects

1. Perspective and point of view are essential to understanding any literary text. Instead of focusing on Noah, think of Allie and consider the events that transpire in *The Notebook* from her perspective. Then prepare an argument in which you make the case for Allie being considered the protagonist of *The Notebook* instead of Noah. Be sure to discuss the thematic significance of such an interpretation.

2. In the first chapter the narrator provides the option of considering *The Notebook* either a love story or a tragedy. Make a two-column chart in which you list all the elements of *The Notebook* that could be considered a love story on one side and all the tragic elements of *The Notebook* on the other. Study the list and determine which side more fully captures the essence of the novel. Write a memo to the advertising department of the book's publisher explaining your decision, which will obviously affect the way the book is marketed to the public. After receiving the memo, assume the role of an advertiser. Prepare a marketing campaign for *The Notebook*. Consider purpose, audience, and mode of communication. Be sure to develop a multi-media ad campaign.

3. Sparks' novel is rich in detail about things that are common in North Carolina. Consider how these details help develop characters, particularly Noah. Then consider how these details affect thematic development. Finally, create a display of things that are unique to the area in which you live. How would these things help outsiders understand you?

CliffsNotes Resource Center

The learning doesn't need to stop here. CliffsNotes Resource Center shows you the best of the best—links to the best information in print and online about the author and/or related works. And don't think that this is all we've prepared for you; we've put all kinds of pertinent information at www.cliffsnotes.com. Look for all the terrific resources at your favorite bookstore or local library and on the Internet. When you're online, make your first stop www.cliffnotes.com where you'll find more incredibly useful information about Sparks' *The Notebook*.

Books and Periodicals

This CliffsNotes book provides a meaningful interpretation of *The Notebook*. If you are looking for information about Nicholas Sparks, check out these other publications:

Cohen, Adam Buckley. "Heroes of Running 2008: The Philanthropist: Nicholas Sparks." *Runner's World,* November 1, 2008.

Gaston, Elaine. "Sparks Writes about Life Choices." *The Sun News* (Myrtle Beach), September 23, 2007.

"Nicholas Sparks." *Contemporary Authors: New Revision Series.* Volume 151. Detroit: Thomson/Galem 354-359.

"Nicholas Sparks, Author of *Nights in Rodanthe* and *The Notebook*." *The Washington Post,* September 17, 2008.

"Sparks, Nicholas." *2001 Current Biography Yearbook.* New York: The H. W. Wilson Company, 511-514.

Sparks, Nicholas. *The Notebook.* (1996). New York: Warner Books, 2004.

Valby, Karen. "True Believer." *Entertainment Weekly.* September 10, 2008, pp. 38-42.

It's easy to find books published by Wiley Publishing, Inc. You can find them in your favorite bookstores (on the Internet and at a store near you). We also have three Web sites that you can use to read about all the books we publish:

- `www.cliffsnotes.com`

- `www.dummies.com`

- `www.wiley.com`

Internet

Check out these Web resources for more information about Nicholas Sparks and *The Notebook:*

"Nicholas   Sparks   Homepage": `http://www.nicholassparks.com`

"Reading   Group   Guide":   `http://www.reading-groupguides.com/guides3/notebook1.asp`

"Bookreporter: Nicholas Sparks Interview": `http://www.bookreporter.com/author/au-sparks-nicholas.asp`

Warner Brothers' *The Notebook* at `www.warnerbros.com`: Search for *The Notebook* on this site, and you can watch the movie trailer and download a version of the poster, a screensaver, and other fun accessories.

Films and Other Recordings

Message in a Bottle, Warner Brothers, 1999. A feature film based on the novel, starring Kevin Costner, Robin Wright Penn, and Paul Newman.

A Walk to Remember, Warner Brothers, 2002. A feature film based on the novel, starring Mandy Moore and Shane West.

The Notebook, New Line Cinema, 2004. A feature film based on the novel, starring Ryan Gosling, Rachel McAdams, James Garner, and Gena Rowlands.

The Notebook. Audio CD. Hachette Audio; Unabridged edition (November 13, 2007).

Nights in Rodanthe, Warner Brothers, 2008. A feature film starring Richard Gere and Diane Lane.

Send Us Your Favorite Tips

In your quest for knowledge, have you ever experienced that sublime moment when you figure out a trick that saves time or trouble? Perhaps you realized you were taking ten steps to accomplish something that could have taken two. Or you found a little-known workaround that achieved great results. If you have discovered a useful tip that helped you study more effectively and you want to share it, the CliffsNotes staff would love to hear from you. Go to our Web site at www.cliffs notes.com and click the Talk to Us button. If we select your tip, we may publish it as part of CliffsNotes Daily, our exciting, free e-mail newsletter. To find out more or to subscribe to a newsletter, go to www.cliffsnotes.com on the Web.

Index

A

"A person can get used to anything, if given
    enough time.", 58
acceptance, 16
Allie. *See* Nelson, Allison
altruistic love, 31
Alzheimer's, 17
Anne. *See* Nelson, Anne
At First Sight, 3
author. *See* Sparks, Nicholas

B

Battle of the Bulge, 20
beauty, 46
Bend in the Road, A, 3
blue-chip stock, 16
book resources, 60
"Bookreporter: Nicholas Sparks Interview", 61
"Break Break Break" poem, 25
Bridges of Madison County, The, 6
Byron, Lord, 45

C

Calhoun, Noah
    "A person can get used to anything, if
        given enough time., 58
    attitude, 22
    character analyses, 52
    "For at that moment, the world is full of
        wonder as I feel her fingers reach for
        the buttons on my shirt and slowly,
        ever so slowly, she begins to undo them
        one by one.", 58
    overview, 9
    real life parallels, 52
    "You can't live your life for other
        people. You've got to do what's right
        for you, even if it hurts some people
        you love.", 58
career highlights, author, 3–4
Cassavetes, Nick, 29

characters
    Allison (Allie) Nelson, 9, 52
    Anne Nelson, 10, 53
    Dr. Barnwell, 10
    Fin and Sarah, 10
    Gus, 10
    Janice, 10
    Lon, 10, 53
    Morris Goldman, 10
    Noah Calhoun, 9, 52
Choice, The, 3
Clare, John, 45
"Clear Midnight, A" poem, 23
Clementine, 18
cliffnotes.com, 60
cliffnotes resource center, 60–61
co-dependent relationship, 32
Cohen, Adam Buckley, 60
commentary, critical. *See* critical commentary
common man, 16, 52
Contemporary Authors: New Revision Series, 60
"Continuities", 47
conversational tone, 15
courtrooms, critical commentary, 38
creek image, 49
critical commentary
    courtrooms, 38
    crossroads, 40
    dedication, 13
    ghosts, 18–26
    kayaks and forgotten dreams, 32–33
    letter from yesterday, 41
    miracles, 13–17
    moving water, 34–35
    phone calls, 31
    reunion, 27–30
    swans and storms, 36–37
    unexpected visitor, 39
    winter for two, 42–50
critical essays
    cliffnotes resource center, 60–61
    fate versus free will, 56
    identifying quotes, 58
    narrative techniques: Sparks' literary
        form, 55
crossroads, critical commentary on, 40

D

Dear John, 3
dedication, critical commentary on, 13
depersonalizing character, 41